counting frogs
and
catching stars

poems by

Jan Woodhouse

yellow
gate
books

Acknowledgements

Poems in this selection have previously been published by Central London Adult Education (*The Water is Wide* and *Considering her Deformity*), Pyramid Press (*Portrait of an Unknown Woman*) and Darius (*The Cat's Fine*). *Considering her Deformity* was reproduced as part of an article on adult education in The Times Educational Supplement. *God's Day Off* was published on My Writing World website.

For feedback and encouragement, thanks, over the years, to the poetry circle at Hereford College; to Bernard Miller's class in London; to the group at Sisterwrite (*Towards a Common Language*); to individuals and friends, and, most recently, to North Norfolk Writers, Poets in the Pub and The Ridge.

Special thanks to Sue Fincham for editorial support with this selection.

ISBN: 0-9553918-0-6
        978-0-9553918-0-4

Published 2006 by:
Yellow Gate Books
5 Greens Road, North Walsham, NR28 0HW
www.yellowgatebooks.com

Printed by ejr print ltd, Norwich

Introduction

My poems have been shaped by a 1950s childhood, and the loosening of taboos and sense of possibility in the 1960s, followed by the women's movement of the 1970s and early 80s, as well as by relationships, encounters, and places lived in. Because of recurring themes, I've placed the poems where they seem to fit rather than in chronological order of writing.

I write primarily to communicate, and I believe my poems work best when my heart, head and guts are equally engaged. It is always good to have positive feedback from other writers, but I am particularly delighted when people who don't normally read or listen to poetry tell me they've been touched by one or other of my poems.

Jan Woodhouse

When I was young, I understood
poems must rhyme, and I knew I could
do it. No sweat. The words would sing
inside my head. This sort of thing -
Forget-me-nots, they are so sweet,
smiling happily in rows so neat.
My mum would smile, and feeling proud,
I'd say it all again out loud -
Forget-me-nots . . . Well, no, not now;
it's not appropriate. Anyhow
years later, sitting alone and drinking
frothy coffee, and quietly thinking
of nothing, I saw across from me
a book called *Modern Poetry*.
And that was my epiphany.

Contents

one...

...Times and places

Bedsitterland

Returning at night
to yet another room that's home for a while
I find myself thinking of all the returnings
to half-familiar wallpaper and beds.

This street could be any street,
that turning any corner.

I look for stars
but there are no stars.
Which way does the moon rise
and where set?

Who might be sleeping now
in beds that I've vacated?

There's the same feeling about
all roads going home at night.

Same feeling about
turning keys and

fighting the draughts of empty rooms
with coffee and transistors.

Back Gardens seen from a Train

Mustn't knock on backdoors
unless they're friends,

so feeling somewhat shameful
I peer through smeary glass
at lines of underwear straddled
across lawns (cared or uncared
for) where abandoned toys lie
scattered.

Boarded-up windows tell the tales
of families moved on. Yet life is
interspersed: a tethered goat; a
black girl playing two-ball; a black
cat poised to spring from an
outhouse roof; and, through an open
door, a woman in a sari in her kitchen.

But the smells of curry and
fish and chips don't reach me.

As children
we would run
to wave at
trains.
The trains
went by. We
stayed and
played.

9

Mornings
(Portrait of the writer as a young mother)

She wakes to a sea of blue –
blue walls, blue quilt,
and a pale shine through
the blue lampshade, misty
like sunrise.

Her baby, with infallible instinct,
swims, mouth open, to her breast.
Sleepily, without effort,
she dispenses stuff that makes him grow.
She is nothing but the sensation
of being sucked. She is not
particularly his mother. No more than
water is mother to weed,
or a tree to moss.

Belly full, he gurgles a smile.
They exchange responses, lying like that
until her three-year-old son bounds in,
a bundle of imperatives:
Come on! Wake up! I want!

He's a creature of games, creations.
His teddy bear's a fish he sails astride
through the waters to some fantasy land.

His energy informs her
that days are for living in.
His happiness in the moment
is unimaginable. His buoyancy
an accusation.

The morning has begun.
She rises, slowly, to its call.

October

The sun shone through mid-afternoon,
a ghost of a day that never was.

I trudged with my son to school,
then back through the mist.

His younger brother sniffed and coughed.
I hugged him close, as though afraid he'd fade.

He laughed at me, all germs and joy.
I watched the dust encircle us

and then got busy with my broom:
shifting, rearranging. Morning

passed that way. We sailed
amongst the mess and toys

and when the sun appeared, I drew the blinds,
not wanting my activity defined.

Evening

Impatiently, I swill the last dishes
in water that needs replacing
because I'm feeling the pull
of the evening.

No stopping me now.
                    I walk
through cow-parsley-scented passages
down to the river, where
hawthorn blossom spills white
against the sunset across the water.

I'm wearing blood red trousers. Birdsong
and my own heartbeat
break into the evening.

I would have gone on down the esplanade,
past the empty factories, only
a man's watching and nervous
I turn around, up the hill, past the flats,
with their effluence of neglect.

Two fifteen-year-olds (thereabouts)
hand me some loose change,
ask me to buy them a bottle of cider.
And because I'm not sure what they'll do
to me if I say no, I do it.

They are all out – the fifteen-year-olds –
doing whatever they find to do
on a Saturday evening in May.

When I was fifteen
I stood on the village green
with my friend, Irene.

We ate chips out of newspaper
and wore net petticoats
to make our skirts stick out.

They billowed as we rode our bikes.
Something was in the air and songs like
dream lover and *all I have to do is dream*
were on our minds.

Nothing much happened, though
I've always kept a space for dreaming.

Gardener's Cottage

You can see me -

tones of grey.
Me with Parents.
Me with Grandfather.
Me with Aunt.

All outside pictures.
We didn't have flash
in those days.

Inside it's shadowy
with what my memory casts.

Grandmother serious and busy.
Bread, cheese and cocoa on the table and
Grandfather having it. Deserving it.
All that hard work he does. Me sitting watching.
Mother behind somewhere and Dad away.

My mind beats wings against a window
in the wild search for coherence
till drained by its efforts it slows
and gives my childhood feet permission
to slip outside. The way they must have.

And things become clearer. Now I find
ants in the cracks. Our lavatory
down the yard, and yellow
newspapers to wipe with.
The smell of paraffin – it would
have been icy in winter.
                                    I don't remember.

My adult mind wants joy, seeks heaven. Whisks
the child to the garden. Not the grey shades of
snapshots but the colours I know. Now. The scents.
The way they mingle.
Look closely -

                                                you can see me.

Off-centre, small and monochrome,
I pick promises like petals.
Watch them fly.

The Tenth of March

Even nature
sometimes slips its seasons.

A chrysalis, misled by the sun,
hatches in January. Or
birds forget to migrate, while others
build nests during a freak mild spell
only to watch them fill with snow.

But today, the tenth of March,
was unofficially, unmistakeably
the first day of spring, after
a dull but unremarkable winter.

To celebrate
I picked my first daffodils.
Put them in a vase with sprigs of
rosemary from the garden
and pussy willow from
alongside the river,
where I saw the first butterflies –
some yellow and a red admiral –
fluttering amongst the dead clusters
of buddleia grown waste and autumn's
old-man's-beard entwining
a wire fence between the river and
the flats, where mothers,
dreary on valium, live cut off
from the river and the life
it flows through.

Yet, today,
as I walked on along the esplanade,
past Blaw Knox and CAV,
people came out in their overalls

to breathe the river, or sit on the bank,
or buy a cornet from the ice-cream van.

       People found time
to celebrate the first day of spring
on the tenth of March

       like me.

From Dublin to Connemara

I met a good man
who took me from
Dublin to Connemara.
He looked after me well.
And often he'd say:

It certainly is definitely without a doubt all right really.

It was like a refrain,
music in my ears.
Whereas I might say,
yes or *mm* or *yeah*
s'pose you're right, he would say:

It certainly is definitely without a doubt all right really.

Does he remember me?
It was a long time ago.
But I remember him
for his kindness, and
the words:

It certainly is definitely without a doubt all right really.

Night Road

I'm remembering how the women
marched with banners: *Reclaim The Night.*
I still have the badge. It's purple
and shiny. And I have the road
to walk down. Dutch courage that warms
my blood. The stars, mysterious
as life. And the dark air, frosty
on skin. Night: simultaneously
intimate and vast. Reclaim me.

So, moving slowly . . .

Rujana and I
shared a room in a Kensington house;
were fed breakfast and prayers
by three Lutheran schwesters in black.
There were others there too.
Young travellers just passing through,
and crazy old women just ending their days there,
and saints who just happened to alight there.
We shared a room for a month.
Rujana of the wild hair and the searching eyes,
who liked to embroider in bed, or to walk in the rain
and the dark, and who said *I will touch first star
when it appears, so to bring luck to you.*

Betty and I
shared lifts in vans and trucks,
places to eat and plates of spaghetti,
and laughs, sweaty cities, Italian men.
She fell in love briefly with one.
Was raped by his friend in a room painted red,
and the sky was cold in the morning we fled to.
We travelled together for a month.
Betty of the long blonde hair and the clear blue eyes.
She told me once what she really wanted
was to find some guy she could settle down with.
She went off on the back of a bike.
Left me on a beach in Corfu, eating
the last of the plums that we'd picked at the roadside.

Antonia and I
shared a basement in Ladbroke Grove.
She loved clothes and food.
She helped me with sewing, and cooked for us both.
I stayed in with her two-year-old son

when she went out at night.
She hated failure;
fantasised about money and love
and when neither came easily,
screamed the place down.
Was rushed off to hospital.
But by then, I wasn't around.
I was expecting a child of my own
and I'd said it was too far to come and babysit.
Proud Antonia of the dark hair and the flickering eyes
whose remembrance is tinged with guilt.

Likewise Olivia.
Olivia and I
shared many a glass of wine and a dream.
Her past, my future, blurring in the telling.
I needed money and she pawned her ring.
Olivia of the grey hair and those sagely blinking eyes.
Her thin wrists bleeding
where she scratched them while she talked
and her loving need to be needed.
For years we kept in touch. She came to stay,
brought wine and talked -
her words becoming vaguer, more repetitive.
I didn't phone for a while, and when I did
she'd moved and moved again –
no one knew where.

Once, many years ago, Rujana sent me a letter
written in green ink. She ended it:
So, moving slowly, I shake your hand, and I move on.

A Norfolk Station on a Winter Evening

It's a matter of absences.
No staff. No ticket machine. No
coffee vendor. No loo. She'll pee
herself in a minute. Come on,
train! No glass in the sides of the
shelter. Must have got smashed. They should
have thought of that. Should have made it
from something more durable. She'll
write a letter to someone. If
she remembers. Tomorrow. My
god, though, doesn't the wind cut to
the bone! No mercy. And what if
the train never comes? What if that
screen that says *on-time-on-time-on-
time* refers to yesterday? Or
the day before. Or no day in
particular. What if it's stuck,
like a needle in the groove of
an old cracked record? What if the
scattered people are just drifters?
Chanced upon this platform like lost
swallows, waiting for time and stars
to re-align. What if that young
woman in the skimpy dress and
strappy sandals has just blown in
from some city street, some hot dry
day? The coat she gathers round her,
a gift from a stranger. The bump
she cradles with her palms, just fruit
of an accidental union
in some half-remembered bed. And
what if the old man, bent and stained,
is dreaming of the smell of roast
chestnuts on a brazier? How he
held his sweetheart's hand. And how the

22

moment glowed. Warm and forever.

What if the train roars by, breathing
steam? Blind to this dereliction
and the figures of its landscape.

December

The wind unravels westwards. A confidence
told to a stranger. Trees bend the other way,
bereft. They know something. So do the birds;
dark silhouettes,

more shadow than substance. If they still sing,
and if I could hear their singing, I think
it would be like those songs that are played
through hollow tubes

in distant wild places. Haunting. And the sun,
when it comes, is just a mirage. Sudden,
blink, gone. Today is almost the shortest
day of the year.

Two . . .

. . . Mostly love

The Water is Wide

At first
I stayed ashore.
I touched the spray and watched
the waves recede.

Then you
calling from somewhere in the distance
shouted 'go'.

I heard
and tentative
I went (and
going
felt the laughter in your voice
knowing
my fear).

I panicked then.

Glanced back at sands
as alien as sea
and dizzy
looked across to where you
(far from me)
kept shouting,
mocking,
'who can't swim!'

Then suddenly

it seemed the laughter wasn't yours

at all.
I saw

you flapping,
sprawling,
just like me.

It seemed

it was the waves that laughed.

Softly without commotion

I like the way
you warm me

gently

moving softly without commotion
beast of the sun.

I like the way
you lead me

gently

talking of friends you have had
and places you have known
and things you have thought

and
talking of various promised lands

while we prowl the crumbling Kensington streets.
And you feed me pretzels on a pub doorstep,
as we down the moment in a pint of ale.

Sunny Sunday mornings.

The wind wafts petals around our feet
and the debris of a Portobello Saturday

as the two of us peer through a shuttered window
at the antiques we can never buy.

I like the way
you light me
gently

as the sun the sea.

I like the way the wind
softly without commotion
wafts our lives
along the Sunday morning streets.

Nothing more to say

Somewhere between the earth and sky
a man in a white crash helmet
wielding his old bike in his own image
blitzes through the ash of other people's dreams.

Friends
delicately sift
the dust

wondering what it was that burned itself out,
and why.

He isn't concerned with their questions.
He has abandoned words for action
(feeling the futility of this, too).

Lovers search his absence for their future,
remembering the warmth
he enjoyed but didn't want,

and wondering who failed, and how,

and sensing that they've somehow missed the point.

Sad, they pick the dust for a few stray sparks
and gently crush them
like shells
in their palms.

Words from Provence

In my *deux étoiles* hotel
I'm happy to be *une*.

I think of you sometimes
when I need to.

When I see lovers.
When I hear love songs.
When I eat in restaurants
and think of how it is
when we eat together
and lie together
and love together.

Other times,
I'm happy
in my own space,
with my own thoughts,
making my own way.

And sometimes,
as I walk,
the words *je t'aime*
are on my breath.

Provence is big enough
to hold them
till I speak to you in English
and we touch in body language.

A skyful of *étoiles*
and you, me, *deux*.

three

Since you've stopped
answering, I've stopped calling,
tossing the reconnection
ball in your court.

I had a dream that the line
was so bad that all I could hear
was a croak, but I knew
it was you, and I tried to say,
Is that you? but I had a bad
throat, and couldn't get it out.

You leave me a message
from another angle to the moon
and your voice caresses me
like the scent of coffee,
like music and comfort,
like breath to skin.

When we're apart

When we're apart
I keep seeing your face
in all the films.

You're always the guy
who gives shit –

the one with
the crooked smile,
the false words –

and one of us always
dies at the end

or we both do.

But in the real world
I find myself
back in your bed
like a frightened child.

So silly.

If there's any saving
to be done, I guess
you're not the one
who's going to be doing it.

I wish, I wish

This morning
you made me feel
like a princess.

From your arms
I danced all the way
to the charity shop

and bought a bagful of
dreams. I wanted to look
beautiful. I wanted to be

your bride in the last scene
of the show, before we both
lived happily ever after.

Three...

...portraits & incidents

Portrait of an Unknown Woman

She paints
her face white,
her lips red.

She dresses with style:
a second-hand outfit
for every occasion.

She steps out briskly,
sometimes skipping
or dancing a bit
along the way.

She talks
to the people
in her head

while the people
in the street
fade to shadows.

She writes her own script.

She doesn't see our disbelief.

What's the point . . ?

What's the point of it all?
he asks, imbibing substances to dumb
the judgement. Head-fucked, out of it. Loose change
is all he asks, still trying to engage
the passing shadows, while his heart grows numb.
Have a nice day, he says.

What's the point of it all?
she wonders, her voice thickened by shouting
and nicotine. Kids, hyper from junk food,
call the shots. She was never one to brood.
Just got on with her life. Now she's doubting.
There must be more, she says.

What's the point of it all?
she yells at the walls of her des res flat.
Her voice bounces back. An echo that taunts
the status she craved, sacrifice made. Haunts
the décor. She knows it's not where it's at.
Love's what we need, she says.

What's the point of it all?
he mumbles. He had a good life, but now,
since Florrie died, the joy's gone out of it.
He makes a cup of tea. Nods off a bit.
Tea's cold. He didn't want it anyhow.
Nothing's the same, he says.

What's the point of it all?
The lilies of the field ask no such thing.
Nor do the sheep that graze, birds of the air,
children absorbed in play. They have no care.
Frowning with concentration, then laughing.
Saying nothing. Having a nice day.

The Crowd Laughs

London. Covent Garden. A hot, late-summer afternoon. A few young men are gathered outside a pub. An old man, one hand clutching a plastic bag, staggers in front of them. One of the young men throws a handful of pennies into the street, and shouts, *Go on, pick them all up.* Still clutching his plastic bag, the old man stoops and gropes for the coins with his other hand. The young men laugh. People look on. They smile.

A car approaches. One of the young men steps out in front of the car and raises his hand, ordering it to stop. The old man copies him. The car stops and waits. The old man continues to scrabble for pennies. As soon as he thinks he has found them all, somebody throws another coin or two, and the old man stoops and scrabbles some more. The car waits. The crowd grows. People laugh.

One woman steps forward from the crowd and shouts at the young men, *I hope you're fucking well ashamed of yourselves.* The young men, and the crowd, pretend they don't hear. More pennies are thrown. The old man stoops and scrabbles. The car waits. The crowd laughs.

The Scream

Last train from Victoria. In the rheumatic clank that passes for silence, people sit, half sleeping, half seeing. Until someone cries a name. *Michael.* An anguished, undulating scream, repeated over and over. And a young woman runs down the train, calling and crying. All the way down the train. Past the scattered, midnight passengers. Down and back. Down and back.

Her companion – a puzzled, pale young man gripping the lead of a scraggy dog – tries to follow her. She doesn't wait. She keeps on running the length of the train and back. Down and back. From time to time she stops. She stops and looks into the eyes of one or other of the passengers. For a moment or two she waits. Wanting something. She stops and then she runs. Down the train and back. Down and back.

The train stops at a station nobody wants to get off at. Two policemen are waiting. They grasp the woman between them, and lead her away. Out of sight. The remaining passengers sit. Say nothing. Look at nobody. And the channel of her running is filled by silence, just as the sifting sand of a dune fills a channel dug by a child's fingers. As if she was never there.

39

The cat's fine

What's it like outside?

Cold, I tell her.
Grey. February slush. Cold,
outside and in.

I'll make a cup of tea.

A smell of gas hovers in the kitchen.
The sink's gunged up with yesterday's dishes.
Leftover catfood rots in a saucer.

The cat sidles up. Yowls.
I open the door to an icy blast.
The cat doesn't go out, yowls some more.
Sod the cat.

I prop her against pillows.
She's light as a child, tiny and wasted
in the double bed. And, at her bedside,
old pension books, empty pill bottles
clutter the passing of time.

I try to ignore the smell from her commode.
Is the cat all right? she asks me.
I tell her, *The cat's fine.*

Her door's always unlocked now.
She lies and watches
day after day
as strangers bustle in and out
loudly, efficiently
making beds, washing dishes,
emptying commodes.
Exuding cheerfulness.

But she no longer has to pretend,
just to submit. Responsible
for no one. Nor herself.

Just, *Is the cat all right?* she asks again.
And again I tell her,
The cat's fine.

God's Day Off (a story)

They called her God.

The name stuck after a comment Marjorie made, in one of her more lucid moments.
'Who does she think she is? God?'

Bert had laughed. Marjorie had laughed too, pleased with herself. Bert was usually so irritable these days.

They were talking about Sandra, the cleaning lady. She was always coming in and telling them what they ought to be doing. Or doing it for them, as if they couldn't be trusted. Changing the bedclothes. Throwing stuff out of the fridge. 'That's *way* past its sell-by-date. And that is. And that is.'

'Here comes God,' Bert would say to Marjorie, when he heard the knock on the door. And they would smile at each other.

One day, though, he didn't say it. He didn't say anything. He couldn't say anything. He was collapsed on the floor.

Marjorie didn't know what to do. God would have known. But God didn't come.

Sandra, the cleaning lady, rang to tell them she wouldn't be coming today; she had a touch of flu. But nobody answered the telephone.

Marjorie couldn't answer the telephone because she'd forgotten how.

Bert couldn't answer the telephone because he was dead.

And Marjorie, still wearing her nightie, because Bert hadn't reminded her to get dressed, went out into the road.

It was a stranger who saw her. The stranger thought something must be amiss, so she asked Marjorie where she was going.

Marjorie thought for a moment. Then she explained:

'I'm looking for God.'

Considering her deformity

She was very lucky
considering her deformity.
She got married.
Had two children.
Both normal.
And she was
quite pretty and she had
her hair done nicely and she wore
nice clothes.
And people sometimes wondered
whether her husband
minded sleeping with a hunchback only
of course being tactful
they never so much as
batted an eyelid to suggest they thought
she wasn't quite normal.

One evening on the Bakerloo Line
(and it had been an ordinary day gone smoothly
enough)
she found herself sitting facing a woman with a
squashed-up nose.
And so
to the horror and amazement of all the other
passengers
(who tactfully continued to stare expressionlessly into
the opposite faces)
she jumped up and gripped the squashed-nosed
woman hard around the neck because
what the hell did she suppose she was doing
being so ugly in a public tube.

Four...

...counting frogs

Monologue heard during a hitched lift

Why be sentimental
when what's gone's gone
like the Sunday joint?
What's pain in a piece of meat? -
he asked, rhetorically,
having just done a post-mortem on a pig.

I was brought up on a farm – he said –
and that's all they are, these creatures.
Meat. And that's all we are, too,
when all's said and done.

Meat.   He prodded his thigh
as we pulled out into the fast lane.

I saw it
pink and limp
beneath the cleaver of his mind.

Stone in my Shoe

I tried to ignore it.
Such a silly thing to have to do:
stop and empty a shoe.

But I had to.
And out it fell
I suppose
though I didn't see it.

Such a speck
to eat into my skin
like a knife.

When I was a child
it was always happening.
'Stop, there's a stone in my shoe'
I would call to the impatient back
of a grown-up.

Sometimes it happened
three times in a day.

Once I let it stay
and ended up with a blister
twenty times stone-size.

Such a speck.
Such a hurt.
Such a tiny speck
and such a big big hurt.

A Child I Lay

A child, I lay
in bed in the dark
thinking of my friend
crying, and how her tears,
in giant waves, rocked
inside me.

In pyjamas I lay
and clutched my hot water bottle
- shaped like a clown and
smelling of rubber –

a raft in an ocean
of feelings
I couldn't understand.

Anybody Screaming

I just heard
a scream in the wind.

Was it a cat
caterwauling?

Or my neighbour
going into labour?

Or someone
being raped
or beaten
or both?

Or was it
something struggling
in my mind?

It might have been
a child crying out in sleep.

Might have been
anybody screaming.

Might just have
been the wind.

Secret Love

I was seduced by - no, entranced
by - women of beauty. On the stage,
they wished and hoped, they sang and danced.
Their dreams came true, they got their man,

the prince. Who left me cold. Was quite
uncharming. I fell for Cinderella.
I gazed and gazed at her until
eyes met. Hers, mine. I took that moment

home. Dreamed, and forgot. Returned
to childish things. Then Sheila wore
a beautiful blue dress in the
school show I wasn't chosen for,

and sang, better than Doris Day,
how *once I had a secret love*. At
ten years old, what did we know
of love? Yet something flipped me

inside-out. The gut-wrench of a song.
Electric blue. Transformed, transfixed.
I know I should know better now,
yet stay complicit in old tricks

that still make magic. Turn down the lights
and start the music. Raise the curtain.
Dress like a princess. Shimmer and sing
like a star. You'll have me spellbound.

Definition of a Bus

You wait for a bus until it comes.
You get on it, and it goes
to where you want to go,
then you get off.

That's one definition.

But I remember a newspaper
headline I saw as a child:
Woman grabs brake as bus-driver dies.
(I kept my eye on drivers for a while,
after that.)

And then there was the man I heard about
who didn't open his mouth for the singing
on the old folks' trip.

Nowadays, sometimes people plant
bombs on buses, the way
we plant hyacinth bulbs in the dark
and wait for what's going to happen,
only quicker.

Sometimes people die on buses.
And that's another definition.

The Maddox Baby is Dead

As usual, I went to call
for my friend to play, but
her curtains were drawn.

The sun was shining.
I knocked, and she came
to the door, and her face
was hushed.

The Maddox baby is dead,
she said.

I looked at the opposite house.
The curtains were drawn. And all
the neighbours' curtains were drawn.

In the morning, she said,
he was here in the street with his mum.
In the afternoon he was dead.

I looked at the street.
The sun shone.
And we and one parked car
were all that was there.

And I don't remember
whether we played, or what.

I only remember the curtains all drawn
and a hush in the sunshine.

Child Size

A summons: 'Can I have a word?'
Punch in the gut. What have I done?
That old refrain echoes. Repeats
to the beat of an old steam train.
What-have-I-done? What-have-I-done?
Truth is, there is no knowing. None.
And innocence cries in silence.
It always did. See how your suit
and heels crumble to dust like a
midnight ball-gown. Your grown-up clothes
ephemeral as make-believe.
Tears in the corridor, the bed.
Back where you came from. It's not *fair*,
you tell them. Those ghosts from your past,
who haunt but don't hear. Never did.

Connections

1

HMS Sheffield sunk in the Atlantic.
Lives lost. Families bereaved.

Meanwhile
we had our local tragedy:
two six-year-old boys,
out fishing with a homemade net,
gone since Monday.

One of them was in my own son's class.
A pale-faced boy with long fair hair
whose dad walked him to school.

First body found
washed-up
on Friday.

Could have been mine,
we mothers think.
Think twice now
when our sons go out to play.

2

He puffs pipe smoke in my face
and when I complain, he says,
'Get out and walk then
if you don't bloody well like it.'

I leave the boxes of shopping
in the boot of his Cortina,
walk home by the river

and try to think of bodies,
but see only life:

ducks wading through mud;
children playing football
(but not those who were lost);
the slow passage of boats.

Would they have grown up
to be men puffing smoke?
Or men fighting in wars?

3

I provoke,
he says.

My words little pellets
aimed below the belt.

I aim them well.
What else am I to do?

When days pass slow
as boats on the water
till death or deaths
scatter the surface calm.

Ex

Mutual neediness wearied us. Daily
we talked without much listening,
while, through my inner ear, the rasp
of my own words echoed,
dreary as solitude.

Was I the one who killed you?
Or the whisky? Something happened.
Your voice faded. Fast. Flesh shrunk,
you sank into your sofa. Unread newspapers
grew daily at your side. Their tower
dwarfed you. All that curiosity and anger
ebbed to a sigh.

I hope it all works out for you

were the last words you said to me.
And something clicked. A light.
Perhaps for the first time
we saw each other clearly.

Monkhopton

I was never there in the frog season
though my mother told me about it.
Squashed frogs all across the road.
You had to tread on them
walking to school and back.

Bad enough to see
one squashed frog
flat in the street;
its guts rolled out like puke.

We used to visit Monkhopton.
Peep through the window
of my mother's old school.
Pick primroses. Picnic.
It was a treat.

If I'd been there in the frog season
I'd probably have had nightmares.
Squashed frogs in my pillow.

In Italy once
I watched a man set fire to a frog.
A scorching afternoon.
A man with a match.
I should have stopped him. Not run.

Before my mother died
I could have asked her:
Remember the picnics?
The primroses?

And now I'm still counting
frogs in my pillow.

Lost Cat

I keep tripping over the space
where he isn't. Hearing the ghost
of a miaow. The click of the cat-flap
suddenly more wanted than Xmas

cards that come with the season. I see
a dark shadow on the carpet, think
it's him, remember. It's like what
happens in bereavement, when a

departed figure resurrects itself
in a million strangers. It's the
irritation I miss. His way of
jumping the queue of my mental

priorities. ME-NOW. I need
the nip of teeth on calf when, stubborn,
I turn my back. Now, I say to the space
that shadows me, now, if you come back,

I'll give you everything you want.
Ten feeds a day. Or more. A lap
that's ever ready. Anything. Share
of my turkey. My pudding. My bed.

Found Cat

And then, a surprise. Black fur, in
a heap, exhausted but fine, it seems.
Purring. Till I see the paw, bent
and spent. The tail that hangs,

redundant. If cats could talk,
he might recount the horror. How,
through two sub-zero nights, he made
it home. If cats could understand

my words, I would tell him why
I need to betray his homecoming;
the bundled rush to have him stood
on a table. Poked and prodded,

drugged and X-rayed. I could have bribed
him with promises of a happy ending
that will come true, more or less,
as he starts to recover the body

he had. Or most of it. And he might
say, Do drunks stop drinking after yet
another fall? Do climbers stop
and rest forever in green valleys?

The Birds

A spider in the bath is one thing.
Bugs in the bed another. But *birds*,
two of them, flying all over the place,
is something scary. OK, God knows
those birds are more afraid than I am,
probably. But then, did I ask them to come
scuttering down the chimney? Like Santas,
out of season, scattering ancient soot.

                                       Woken
by sounds that weren't the alarm, cat-flap,
footsteps, loo chain, etcetera, but had to be
*in*side, not out, I shouted *What's that noise?*
Refusing to get up before I knew. It's *birds*.
I felt like Tippi Hedren, the way those wings
can come at you. Even the cat fled. I froze.
Cataplexy.

                          Luckily, unlike wasps,
birds know an open window when they
see one. Rocket to safety of sky.
Leaving the house suddenly birdless,
and me up-ending vases, sponging
shit from cushions. Making things normal.

Five . . .

. . . catching stars

Sometimes

Sometimes I don't need much
in the way of books,
newspapers, conversation.

Sometimes
my own thoughts
are enough,
filling my mind the way
a womb fills up and swells
in pregnancy.

Sometimes
I think of people and places
I've known and maybe loved
and I want to fly through
whatever dimensions of space and time
might take me to them,
just so I can say 'hello'.

And other times
my mind's both light and heavy
with all my past contains, and more.

And I don't need to fly.
Don't even need to think very much.
Just let the flow of places and lovers
rise and ebb
in the warmth of sun on flesh,
ripples of breeze and birdsong,
the distant roar of traffic,
and the love I feel for
whoever might be loveable and around.
Indolence
has its own momentum;
is an experience no less valid

than adventure or an affair,
and is not loveless.

Sometimes
my own company
is enough.

Sunflowers in October

Our garden's full
of sunflowers.
They sway and straggle
bowed by wind and
drenched by rain.

Belated suns
in a tangle of
greenery.

My son took seeds
from the hamster feed,
and planted them
one by one.

I said
it was too late.
They'd never flower.

They've proved me wrong.

     Tall
        stalks
            racing

                the onrushing darkness,
                the imminent winter.

Snowball

The sky and the horizon
blur, white fading into white.
Easy to comprehend how

the earth is round, like a ball
of snow, rolling and rolling,
gathering more of itself

along the way, so that the
things we normally see are
lost entirely to this

overwhelming whiteness. And
it doesn't seem too far-fetched
to wonder whether, if we

keep rolling, on and on, we'll
soon become layered so deep,
and lose our boundaries so

completely, that when it all
melts, eventually, we'll find
ourselves resurfacing, not

with the people we thought we
knew, but the people we might
have known, in another life,

somewhere, before circumstance
blinded us with illusion;
threw us up here and not there.

Faces

Faces come and go
and some come back

and some come back the same
and we don't know them

and some come back changed
and we nod in recognition

and we become once more like children
not stopping too long to worry too much
what's right, what's real

Last seen walking in mountains

The helicopter hovers. Whirrs. Won't go away.
Circles. Keeps coming back.
And I start to feel like a naughty child
caught by God, who sees everything.
Even our thoughts and our dreams.

They're like parents, like governments, those guys.
Always keeping an eye.
Shall I give them a surprise?
Strip off in the cold mountain air. Let the wind
blow my pubes. Wave my Medusa hair.

Silly cow, they'll be saying.
Their last words, cast in stone,
in the sky. And me, laughing.
Free as a cloud.

On reading obituaries

I have my own dead friends – I don't want more,
and yet I can't help finding myself drawn
to those lives departed. What they stood for.
The essence of them. Of course, they were born,
they died, as we all were and will. It's what
is remembered of them, in the end, though,
that counts. Their actions, beliefs. Words. It's not
their doubts, their fears. The roads not taken. Show
me a life lived well, and bravely. Play me
the lyrics, and I'll catch the tune. The moon
must smile, though, to see the shadowy spaces,
unwritten. The dreams. The secret places.

Elements

I would gaze at the night sky
waiting for a tiny star
to fall at my feet
in their sensible Startrite shoes.

I would scoop sand in my palms,
let it slide through my fingers.
Discover treasure:
scalloped, smooth, tinted or glistening.

I would watch as ripples of life
wakened a pond's still silence.
See magic forests
in the haphazard dance of flames.

Though people say differently,
we *can* go back. Find wonder
in small or big things.
Leave explanation to grown-ups.

Blow seed heads.
Send wishes.
Unlearn war games.
Imagine.

(with acknowledgement to John Lennon for the last word)

Poems listed in order of time written:

1960s
Bedsitterland, The Water is Wide, Considering her deformity, Monologue heard during a hitched lift

1970s
Mornings, October, Softly without commotion, Nothing more to say, Faces

1980s
Back Gardens seen from a Train, Evening, The Tenth of March, So moving slowly, The cat's fine, A Child I Lay, Anybody Screaming, The Maddox Baby is Dead, Connections, Sometimes, Sunflowers in October

1990s
Words from Provence, three, When we're apart, I wish I wish, Portrait of an Unknown Woman, The Crowd Laughs, The Scream, Stone in my Shoe, Monkhopton

2000-2006
Gardener's Cottage, From Dublin to Connemara, Night Road, A Norfolk Station on a Winter Evening, December, What's the point . . . ?, God's Day Off, Secret Love, Definition of a Bus, Child Size, Ex, Lost Cat, Found Cat, The Birds, Snowball, Last seen walking in mountains, On reading obituaries, Elements